AT A PARTICULAR AGE:

HEAVY SNOW REVISITED

BY JOHN HAUGSE

To order additional copies of this book, contact:
Xlibris
1-888-795-4274
www.Xlibris.com
Orders@Xlibris.com

ISBN: Softcover 978-1-7960-9662-0
          Hardcover 978-1-7960-9663-7
          EBook   978-1-7960-9661-3

Library of Congress Control Number: 2020907253

Print information available on the last page

Rev. date: 07/27/2020

This book is dedicated to all those
who commit their lives to the service of others.

At a Particular Age: Heavy Snow Revisited is the story of a son taking care of his father who is slowly and painfully disappearing into Alzheimer's disease. Through the illustrated-vignette style of the book the author portrays with poignancy and humor the tragedy of Alzheimer's and the terrible strain it puts on the caregiver, family and friends. The son's disturbing dream sequences reveal the psyche and the hidden fears we all have about this frightening disease. While the story focuses on the care of an Alzheimer's sufferer, it is also the story of how an estranged father and son are brought together by illness. For over forty years the conservative minister father and the artist son have had a relationship based on conflict and anger, By caring for his father the son hopes to resolve their bitter difficulties and find peace before the disease makes it impossible.

TABLE OF CONTENTS

FOREWORD

IN 1998 MY FATHER DIED OF ALZHEIMER'S DISEASE. I HAD BEEN HIS GUARDIAN FOR THE 6 YEARS THAT LED UP TO HIS DEATH. I'M A PAINTER AND ANIMATOR BY TRAINING, SO IT WAS NATURAL THAT I WOULD KEEP A VISUAL RECORD OF THOSE TIMES.

AFTER HIS DEATH I USED THAT MATERIAL TO WRITE THE ORIGINAL VERSION OF THIS STORY WHICH WAS PUBLISHED IN 1999. I CALLED IT

HEAVY SNOW: MY FATHER'S DISAPPEARANCE INTO ALZHEIMER'S

I AM NOW AT THE AGE HE WAS WHEN HIS TROUBLE STARTED SO IT SEEMED PARTICULARLY IMPORTANT THAT AFTER 20 YEARS I MIGHT HAVE SOME NEW INSIGHTS ON THAT EXPERIENCE.

What I mean, of course, is now that I'm the age he was when all this started I can draw and write more freely

and without the feeling that he is looking over my shoulder.

2019 John Haugse ©

4

DAD LEARNING HOW TO HELP, BEING HELPED.

9

BY THE TIME HE WAS IN GRADE SCHOOL HE HAD PRETTY MUCH DECIDED HOW HE'D SPEND HIS LIFE.

BORN IN THE MID-WEST TO WORKING CLASS NORWEGIAN IMMIGRANTS. HE WAS THE FIRST OF HIS FAMILY TO GO TO COLLEGE.
HE IMAGINED HIMSELF LIVING THE LIFE OF A BACHELOR, DEDICATED TO STUDY AND SERVICE. A LUTHERAN MONK.

..BUT HE HAD NOT ALLOWED FOR THE YOUNG GIRL'S SCARF OR THE PLAYFUL LOOK SHE GAVE HIM.

..And all that follows..

and so
the story
begins

MY FATHER RAISED THREE CHILDREN, COACHED A BASKETBALL TEAM, PERFORMED BAPTISMS, WEDDINGS, FUNERALS AND WROTE A NEW SERMON EVERY FRIDAY. HE ACHIEVED THE RANK OF LT. COL. IN THE ARMY RESERVES. HE WENT OFF TO WAR IN THE PACIFIC WHEN I WAS FIVE.

AFTER THE WAR WE MOVED OUT WEST AND STARTED OUR LIVES OVER.

AS THE YEARS PASSED, THE CLOSENESS I'D HAD WITH MY FATHER CHANGED.
WHY DOES IT ALWAYS RAIN WHEN I WANT TO PLAY OUTSIDE?
GOD
WHY?
GOD
GOD
?
GOD
WHY ARE YOU WASTING ALL YOUR TIME DRAWING THESE PICTURES WHEN YOUR GRADES ARE SO LOW?
WHAT ARE THEY TEACHING YOU IN THAT HIGH SCHOOL? COMMUNISM?
IT'S GREAT MUSIC.
SOVIET ARMY
YOU'RE NOT GOING DRESSED LIKE THAT ARE YOU?
OF COURSE NOT
MY SON, THE THE BEATNIK

I left for college in 1956.

AS SOON AS I COULD I DECLARED MYSELF AN ART MAJOR.

AFTER SEVEN YEARS OF COLLEGE AND TWO DEGREES, I WAS PAINTING FULL TIME AND EARNING A MEAGER LIVING AS A FRAME MAKER.

I LEARNED ZEN, WHICH MY FATHER REFERRED TO AS PART OF AN ANTI-CHRIST MOVEMENT.

ISN'T THIS A GREAT PICTURE OF JOHN AND JILL IN THE PARADE?

18

THE DISTANCE BETWEEN MY FATHER AND I GREW UNTIL IT SEEMED LIKE WE WERE ON OPPOSITE SIDES OF EVERY ISSUE FACING THE COUNTRY.

Over the years

we set our jaws and

lost sight of each other.

SIGNS OF TROUBLE

MY FATHER WAS DIAGNOSED WITH ALZHEIMER'S DISEASE WHEN HE WAS IN HIS EARLY 80'S. HE HAD RECENTLY RETIRED FROM THE LUTHERAN CHURCH AS ONE OF THEIR "HOME MISSIONS" PASTORS. NO DOUBT, HIS SYMPTOMS HAD LONG PROCEEDED THE ANNOUNCEMENT, BUT WHERE BAD NEWS IS CONCERNED, IT IS ALWAYS BEST TO PUT IT OFF AS LONG AS POSSIBLE. AND SO THE REALITY OF HIS CONDITION CAME TO US IN BITS AND PIECES, AS IT DOES TO MOST FAMILIES.

YOU WON'T BELIEVE WHAT'S HAPPENING WITH DAD, HE FORGETS EVERYTHING ALMOST RIGHT AWAY. YESTERDAY I FOUND HIM AT 3 IN THE MORNING IN THE GARAGE LOOKING FOR HIS MONKEY WRENCH.

MY WIFE AND I HAD BEEN CONSIDERING MOVING TO THE NORTHWEST. MY FOLKS LIVED IN WASHINGTON, SO WE STAYED WITH THEM WHILE WE LOOKED FOR A PLACE.

MOM WAS WORRIED AND WANTED TO TALK, BUT WHATEVER WE SUGGESTED WAS MET WITH A GRACIOUS, BUT FIRM REFUSAL.

DO YOU THINK THIS MEMORY THING WITH DAD IS SERIOUS OR IS MOM OVER REACTING?

WELL, HE DOESN'T ALWAYS REMEMBER WHO I AM.

ANYWAY, I'M GLAD MOM'S AROUND TO TAKE CARE OF HIM.

MMMMM

ALTHOUGH WE DIDN'T TALK ABOUT IT MUCH, WE KNEW THAT MY FOLKS WERE GETTING TO THE AGE WHEN THEY WOULD NEED MORE ATTENTION AND HELP FROM US.

WE MOVED TO PORTLAND, A TWO HOUR DRIVE FROM MY PARENTS' HOME IN WASHINGTON.

SHORTLY AFTER WE SETTLED IN, I DROVE UP TO VISIT THEM. MOM SENT US ON AN ERRAND.

27

MOM STEALS HOME

I WAS WORKING LATE ON AN ANIMATION ASSIGNMENT WHEN DAD CALLED.

34

LATE THAT AFTERNOON MOM TOOK A TURN FOR THE WORSE, I CALLED MY BROTHER BILL AND SISTER RUTH AND SETTLED DOWN TO WAIT.

BY THE TIME EVERYONE GOT TO THE HOSPITAL, MOM'S CONDITION WAS CRITICAL. WE TOOK TURNS GRABBING NAPS. A BASEBALL GAME BLARED ON THE TELEVISION IN THE WAITING ROOM.

37

WHO GETS DAD?

39

HIS "ATTACK" TURNED OUT TO BE NERVES AND AN ACID STOMACH. THE FUNERAL WAS HELD WITHOUT DAD.

DAD'S MOODS CHANGED RAPIDLY AND WITHOUT WARNING.

WORRIED THAT THERE WAS NO ONE TO LOOK AFTER HIM, I SPOKE TO MEMBERS OF HIS CHURCH WHO ASSURED ME THAT THEY WOULD TAKE GOOD CARE OF HIM.

IT WAS THE PERFECT SOLUTION. I HAD ABSOLVED MYSELF OF RESPONSIBILITY AND GIVEN IT TO OTHERS.

IT SOON BECAME CLEAR THAT DAD COULD NOT LIVE IN THE HOUSE BY HIMSELF.

DAMN
DAMN
DAMN

45

TAKING CHARGE

NEARLY EVERYONE SPOKE TO HIM ABOUT SELLING THE HOUSE AND MOVING TO AN ASSISTED CARE HOME, BUT IT WASN'T UNTIL THE BISHOP VISITED THAT HE BEGAN TO ACCEPT THE IDEA.

THE HOUSE SOLD EASILY. MOVING DAD WAS THE HARD PART.

49

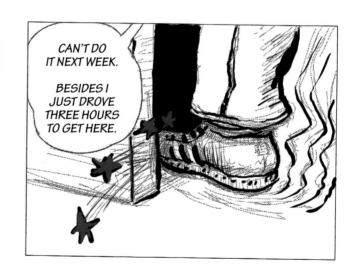

WE NEVER MENTIONED HIS MEMORY LOSS AGAIN OR SAID THE WORD, ALZHEIMER'S.

FINALLY, ALL THESE BOOKS ARE IN BOXES.

WHO KEEPS PUTTING ALL MY BOOKS IN BOXES?

I KNOW THAT MAKING THIS MOVE WITHOUT MOM IS GOING TO BE DIFFICULT, BUT YOUR NEW APARTMENT WILL HAVE PEOPLE TO HELP BLAH BL

WE HAD WANTED TO GET DAD INTO AN ASSISTED LIVING ENVIRONMENT, BUT HE WOULDN'T HEAR OF IT. INSTEAD WE FOUND A SPACE FOR HIM IN A RETIREMENT FACILITY WITH NURSING AIDES ON STAFF.

CHECK AND MATE

HE CAN'T FIND HIS WAY HOME FROM THE STORE, BUT HE STILL BEATS ME EASILY AT CHESS. GO FIGURE.

REALIZING THAT DAD WOULD NEVER WILLINGLY MOVE OUT OF HIS HOUSE, I TOOK A FEW OF HIS THINGS AND MADE IT AS HOMEY AS POSSIBLE.

I DROVE HIM TO HIS NEW HOME AND INTRODUCED HIM TO THE STAFF. WHILE THEY WERE SETTLING HIM IN I WENT BACK TO FINISH PACKING.

BY THE TIME I RETURNED, DAD WAS ASLEEP IN HIS CHAIR.
HE NEVER MENTIONED THE HOUSE AGAIN.

DAD'S DRIVING, WHICH HAD BEEN TERRIBLE FOR YEARS, HAD BECOME SERIOUSLY DANGEROUS. IT SEEMED THAT EVERYONE EXPECTED ME TO SOLVE THE PROBLEM.

REASON: *TO THINK, FORM JUDGEMENTS AND DRAW CONCLUSIONS.*

CONFRONT: *TO FACE OR OPPOSE BOLDLY.*

HUMOR: *TO JOKE OR AMUSE.*

FRUSTRATE: *PREVENTED FROM ACHIEVING AN OBJECTIVE.*

LOOKS LIKE YOU'LL HAVE TO RELY ON ME. DAD.

I'LL PRAY FOR BOTH OF US.

WATCH OUT, YOU'RE TOO CLOSE TO THAT GUY. YOU'RE GOING TOO FAST.

COULD YOU GO BACK TO PRAYING FOR US? PLEASE.

IN THE END, IT WAS HIS MECHANIC WHO SOLVED THE PROBLEM BY INSISTING HE KEEP THE CAR IN THE SHOP FOR "BADLY NEEDED REPAIRS".

DAD OCCASIONALLY ASKED ABOUT THE CAR, BUT HE WAS EASILY DISTRACTED. I THOUGHT PERHAPS HE HAD WANTED TO STOP DRIVING BUT HADN'T KNOWN HOW.

HOW YOU FEELING? DAD?

WITH MY FINGERS.

DO YOU REMEMBER IF WE THREW OUT ANYTHING AT ALL?

DON'T BE A SMART ALECK

ONCE THE ISSUES OF THE HOUSE AND CAR WERE RESOLVED, DAD SEEMED TO RELAX AND BE MORE LIKE HIS OLD SELF. I BEGAN TO THINK THAT MAYBE HIS MEMORY PROBLEMS HAD BEEN MY IMAGINATION AFTER ALL.

60

LOSING GROUND

I THINK YOU'LL BE PLEASED WHEN YOU SEE HOW WELL HE'S DOING.

OH, OH

SEVERAL MONTHS LATER, MY SISTER RUTH VISITED. I WAS EAGER FOR HER TO SEE HOW WELL DAD WAS DOING.

SOMEHOW HE'D MANAGED TO GET ALL HIS BOXES OUT OF STORAGE AND INTO HIS APPARTMENT.

YOU GO FIND DAD. I'M GOING TO DO SOME CLEANING UP.

I HAVE A SURPRISE FOR YOU, DAD.

THIS IS A BARBER SHOP AND YOU'RE GOING TO GET A HAIRCUT?

WHO?

RUTH, SISTER RUTH.

RUTH, I'M GLAD YOU'RE HERE. YOU WOULDN'T BELIEVE HOW THEY TREAT ME HERE. THEY WAKE ME AT ALL HOURS OF THE NIGHT. THEY STEAL MY THINGS. JOHN STEALS FROM ME TOO.

I'M SURE HE DIDN'T RECOGNIZE ME AT FIRST.

HE WAS JUST STRESSED OUT WHEN HE COULDN'T FIND ANYTHING.

HE NEEDS TO HAVE HIS THINGS OUT WHERE HE CAN SEE THEM. OTHERWISE HE FORGETS WHERE THEY ARE.

ONCE AGAIN WE HAD TO FIND ANOTHER LIVING ARRANGEMENT FOR DAD. THE FIRST STEP WAS A DOCTOR'S EVALUATION.

DAD AGREED TO SEE A DOCTOR, BUT ONLY ON THE CONDITION THAT IT BE HIS CARDIOLOGIST, A RETIRED ARMY DOCTOR NOW IN PRIVATE PRACTICE.

IT WAS COMMON FOR MANY DOCTORS TO VIEW DEMENTIA AS JUST A PART OF AGING. THIS HAPPENED A NUMBER OF TIMES BEFORE DAD WAS PROPERLY DIAGNOSED. RUTH ANNOUNCED THAT SHE WAS RETURNING TO HER HOME IN JORDAN.

SINCE RUTH WAS LEAVING THE COUNTRY, I DECIDED TO FIND A FACILITY CLOSER TO PORTLAND.

REMEMBER, IT MAY TAKE A LITTLE TIME TO ADJUST TO THIS NEW ENVIRONMENT.

DAD HASN'T ADJUSTED TO THE FACT THAT HE'S OVER FORTY YET.

WHERE ARE WE SON, TAKE ME HOME.

ACTUALLY I WASN'T REFERRING TO YOUR FATHER.

No Really

THE NEXT MORNING I RETURNED TO THE NURSING HOME, DETERMINED TO OVERCOME MY FEAR OF THIS STRANGE ENVIRONMENT.

YESTERDAY YOU OFFERED TO SHOW ME AROUND THE WARD. DO YOU HAVE TIME TO DO THAT TODAY?

SURE.

LATE THAT EVENING I SIGNED THE ADMITTANCE PAPERS.

RUTH AND I MOVED DAD TO HIS NEW HOME OUTSIDE PORTLAND, OREGON. WE WERE IN GOOD SPIRITS AND SANG THE WHOLE WAY THERE.

WHEN WE GOT TO THE NURSING HOME DAD'S MOOD TURNED UGLY.

Dad giving communion draws a crowd. 1999

IT DROVE THEM CRAZY, HE'D TAKE OFF, WALK TO TOWN THEN REPORT HIS CAR STOLEN OR JUST WALK INTO A BUILDING AND WAIT FOR SOMEONE TO FETCH HIM. MOST EVERYONE GOT TO KNOW HIM DURING THAT TIME AND THOUGHT IT CHARMING, BUT THE STAFF PEOPLE AT THE HOME WERE QUITE UNSETTLED BY IT.

UNABLE TO KEEP HIM FROM LEAVING THE BUILDING THEY FASTENED AN ALARM ONTO THE BACK OF HIS SHIRT, WHICH HE PROMPLY REMOVED AND WALKED OUT THE DOOR WITH THE HELP OF AN UNSUSPECTING VISITOR.

93

DAD SETTLED INTO HIS SITUATION AND WE SETTLED INTO A ROUTINE. I OFTEN TOOK HIM FOR DRIVES UP THE COLUMBIA RIVER FOR LUNCH. IT WAS ABOUT THIS TIME THAT HE STARTED CLAPPING. I NEVER FOUND OUT WHY, BUT HE WAS ALWAYS SMILING WHEN HE CLAPPED SO I FIGURED IT MEANT HE WAS HAPPY.

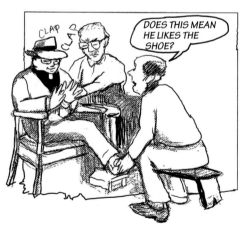

WE BEGAN TO BUILD A NEW RELATIONSHIP BASED ON MY CHILDHOOD EXPERIENCES.

DURING THIS TIME, I TALKED TO DAD IN A WAY I HAD NEVER BEEN ABLE TO BEFORE. HE JUST WHISTLED OR CLAPPED HIS HANDS AND WATCHED ME INTENTLY... BUT THERE WERE ALWAYS SURPRISES.

"Don't know their stories"

ONE WINTER AFTERNOON, I WAS WALKING WITH MY FATHER OUTSIDE HIS NURSING HOME. IT WAS SNOWING HEAVILY. I GLANCED BACK TO LOOK AT OUR TRAIL AND NOTICED THAT HIS TRACKS HAD ALMOST VANISHED WHILE MINE WERE STILL WELL DEFINED. I JOKED WITH HIM ABOUT THIS AND ASKED WHAT HE THOUGHT IT MEANT. HE REPLIED, "I'M NOT SURPRISED, I OFTEN FEEL LIKE I'M DISAPPEARING."

THAT FIRST YEAR IN THE NURSING HOME I TOOK DAD TO CHURCH NEARLY EVERY SUNDAY

A HIGHLIGHT OF GOING TO CHURCH WAS LOOKING AT HIS PICTURE IN THE ENTRY. HE HAD HELPED TO ORGANIZE THE CHURCH AND WAS THE FIRST ORDAINED MINISTER. I'M NOT SURE HOW MUCH OF ALL THAT HE REMEMBERED, BUT HE DEFINITELY RECOGNIZED HIS PICTURE.

COFFEE HOUR AFTER CHURCH WAS A MAJOR PART OF OUR ROUTINE.

IT'S OFTEN DIFFICULT WITH PEOPLE WHO HAVE DEMENTIA, TO DETERMINE WHAT HURTS AND WHY. THAT'S WHY IT'S IMPORTANT TO BE ON THE LOOK OUT FOR POSSIBLE PROBLEMS. MY SISTER WAS MUCH BETTER AT THAT SORT OF THING THAN I.

THE NEXT MORNING A DENTIST PULLED A BADLY IMPACTED MOLAR. DAD REGAINED HIS WEIGHT IN NO TIME.

THANKS DOCTOR, SORRY ABOUT THE FINGER.

DAD, I KNOW YOUR TOOTH FEELS FUNNY, BUT TRY TO KEEP YOUR HANDS OUT OF YOUR MOUTH.

HMMMM, I SEEM TO HAVE LOST MY KEYS.

105

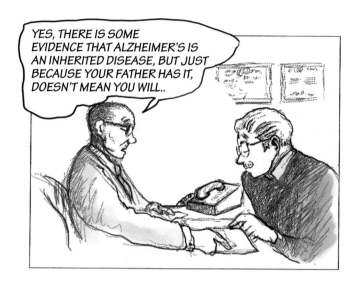

SUSAN

SEVERAL YEARS AFTER ENTERING THE HOME, DAD MET A
NEW RESIDENT, SUSAN. SHE WAS IN HER EARLY 70'S AND
ALSO SUFFERED FROM ALZHEIMER'S DISEASE. THEY BECAME
CONVINCED THAT THEY WERE MARRIED.

THE STAFF REFERRED TO THEM AS, "THE COUPLE", WHICH I SUPPOSED GAVE THEM SOME LEVEL OF STATUS. I WAS IN
FAVOR OF THIS UNION SINCE IT SEEMED TO HAVE A CALMING EFFECT ON DAD WHICH IN TURN MADE MY LIFE MUCH EASIER.
BUT NOTHING IS PREDICTABLE OR LONG LASTING WHEN DEALING WITH DEMENTIA.

I HAD TO ADMIT THAT THEY DID MAKE A CUTE COUPLE. I HAVE NO IDEA WHAT THEY TALKED ABOUT, BUT IT SEEMED INTIMATE AND COMFORTING TO THEM.

SUSAN NEVER REMEMBERED ME SO WE HAD A RITUAL INTRODUCTION ON EACH VISIT.

SUSAN OFTEN JOINED US FOR OUR WALKS, BUT SHE WAS ALWAYS A LITTLE SUSPICIOUS OF ME.

ONE EVENING I GOT A FRANTIC CALL FROM THE NURSING STAFF.

DAD HAD CHASED SUSAN'S ROOMMATES OUT IN ORDER TO GO TO BED WITH HIS "WIFE".

AS YOU SEE IN THESE REPORTS JOHN, THERE ARE A NUMBER OF COMPLAINTS ABOUT YOUR FATHER'S BEHAVIOR BESIDES LAST NIGHT'S INCIDENT.

NATURALLY, I IMAGINED THE WORST. WE SET UP A MEETING FOR THE NEXT MORNING.

BEFORE WE HAD TIME TO COMPLETE THE PAPERWORK, DAD GOT INTO TROUBLE AGAIN.

HE SEEMED PARTICULARLY UPSET BY ONE OF THE PATIENTS ON THE WARD. A YOUNG MAN WHO HE WAS CONVIENCED WAS, "OF THE DEVIL". HE HAD NEVER USED LANGUAGE LIKE THAT BEFORE AND IT WORRIED ME.

IN THE COMPANY OF MEN.

THAT FIRST MORNING IN THE HOSPITAL, I WAS STRUCK BY HOW FRAGILE DAD HAD BECOME AND HOW MUCH HE'D AGED DURING THE LAST FEW YEARS. IT WAS A DIFFICULT TIME FOR BOTH OF US.

THE VA PSYCHIATRIC WARD WAS VERY DIFFERENT FROM THE NURSING HOME, BUT DAD SEEMED TO FIT IN EASILY.

ONCE OFF HIS MEDICATIONS, HE SEEMED TO GET SOME OF HIS HUMOR BACK AND STARTED ACTING HIS OLD SELF AGAIN.

HOW YOU FEELING, DAD?

WITH MY FINGERS.

YOU DON'T WANT ME TO GET WELL.

WHAT DO YOU MEAN BY THAT. OF COURSE I WANT YOU TO GET WELL.

YOU WANT ME TO GET BETTER, BUT YOU DON'T WANT ME TO GET WELL.

WHEN I THOUGHT ABOUT IT, I WASN'T SURE IF I DID WANT HIM TO GET BETTER, IF BY "BETTER", HE MEANT GOING BACK TO THE WAY IT HAD BEEN BETWEEN US. DID HIS DEMENTIA ALLOW HIM SOME NEW INSIGHT, OR WAS THIS JUST ANOTHER RANDOM THOUGHT?

119

ONE EVENING WHILE WE WERE WALKING ON THE GROUNDS OF THE VA HOSPITAL..

YOU'RE PRETTY QUIET TODAY.

WHEN I SPEAK, IT'S LIKE SOMEONE ELSE'S VOICE COMES OUT OF MY MOUTH.

I LOVE YOU, DAD AND I'M SORRY FOR WHAT YOU'RE GOING THROUGH.

I'LL BE ALRIGHT..I'LL BE FINE.

COME ON IT'S GETTING COLD OUT HERE

DAD WAS RELEASED LATER THAT EVENING. HIS MEDICATION WAS EXACTLY WHAT IT HAD BEEN WHEN HE CAME. I KNEW THAT IF HIS BEHAVIOR CONTINUED, I WOULD HAVE TO FIND OTHER LIVING ARRANGEMENT FOR HIM. THE STAFF AT THE NURSING HOME MADE HIM FEEL WELCOME AND IN A SHORT TIME HE SETTLED BACK IN.

AFTER HIS RETURN FROM THE HOSPITAL, HE TOOK LITTLE NOTICE OF SUSAN.

WE CANCELED OUR PLAN TO HAVE THEM SHARE A ROOM.

SLIDING HOME

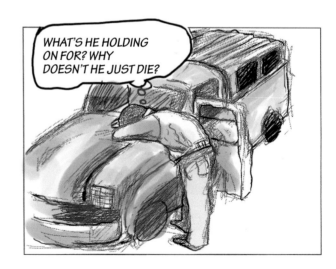

THIS EVENT MARKED A TURNING POINT FOR ALL OF US. THE SPONTANEOUS NATURE OF OUR TRIPS UP THE RIVER AND OUR WEEKLY CHURCH TIME WOULD BE LIMITED. FORTUNATELY RUTH WAS RETURNING AGAIN FROM THE NEAR EAST. I LOOKED FORWARD TO HER CALMING PRESENCE AND HER NURSING EXPERIENCE.

RUTH SLIPPED QUICKLY AND EASILY INTO LOOKING AFTER DAD'S PHYSICAL NEEDS. THIS KINDLY ATTENTION FROM A VAGUELY FAMILIAR FACE WAS A WELCOME CHANGE FOR DAD AND FOR A TIME, IT SEEMED THAT HE WAS GETTING HIS GOOD HUMOR BACK. I FOCUSED ON HIS INCREASING CONFUSION AND THE GROWING DISTANCE BETWEEN US.

DOESN'T IT BOTHER YOU THAT HE DOESN'T ALWAYS RECOGNIZE US?

I GUESS I'M GETTING USED TO IT.

HIS SKIN PROBLEMS ARE MORE IMPORTANT NOW.

HMMM. FIRST I TRADE PLACES WITH MY FATHER, NOW WITH MY SISTER.

(1) SKIN TREATMENT NEXT WED. 4:00. (2) TAKE DAD'S RECORDS.

AS DAD'S DISEASE PROGRESSED TO THE FINAL STAGE AND RUTH TOOK OVER AS CARE MANAGER, I FELT MYSELF PULLING AWAY.

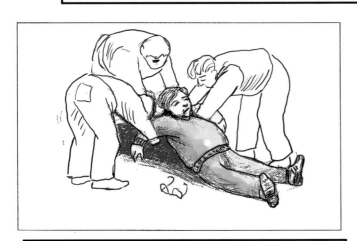

A SHORT TIME LATER, DAD FELL AND BROKE HIS HIP. HE HEALED QUICKLY AND RETURNED TO THE NURSING HOME IN LESS THAN A WEEK.

WE WERE ASSURED THAT BECAUSE OF HIS PHYSICAL STRENGTH HE WOULD EASILY WALK AGAIN.

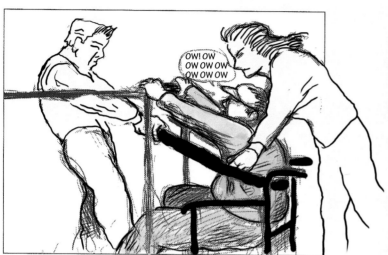

BUT DESPITE ALL EFFORTS, DAD NEVER WALKED AGAIN.

RUTH AND I TRIED EVERYTHING TO ENGAGE HIM, BUT THE GAP BETWEEN US HAD BECOME TOO GREAT.

DAD'S APPEARANCE CHANGED SO QUICKLY DURING THIS TIME THAT ON SEVERAL OCCASIONS, RUTH AND I WALKED RIGHT PAST HIM.

SEVERAL MONTHS AFTER HIS HIP SURGERY, DAD ONCE AGAIN DEVELOPED LOWER INTESTINAL INFECTION. WHICH INVOLVED A LONG RECOVERY.

AFTER CONFERRING WITH HIS DOCTORS RUTH, BILL AND I DECIDED NOT TO HOSPITALIZE DAD AGAIN.

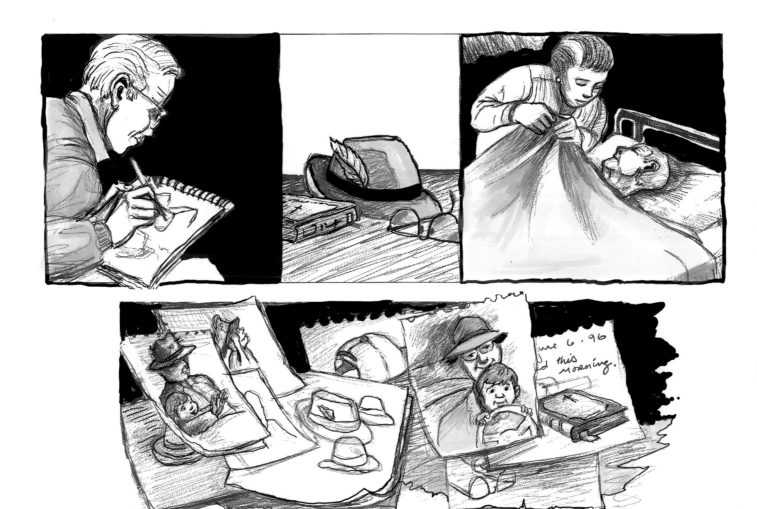

DAD DIED ON A SUNDAY MORNING, SHORTLY AFTER CHURCH. HE HAD LIVED IN THE NURSING HOME FOR A LITTLE OVER SIX YEARS. RUTH AND I SAT NEXT TO HIS BED FOR A LONG TIME. I WONDERED WHAT SHE WAS THINKING, BUT DIDN'T ASK.

IT WAS MONTHS BEFORE I WENT TO THE GRAVESITE. I STOOD STARING AT MY FATHER'S NAME ON THE MARKER, WONDERING WHY WE HADN'T TAKEN THE TIME TO SHORTEN THE DISTANCE BETWEEN US WHEN WE HAD THE CHANCE. ON THE DRIVE HOME, I REALIZED, AT LAST, I WAS GOING TO MISS MY FATHER.

SEVERAL YEARS LATER, MY SISTER RUTH WAS DIAGNOSED WITH EARLY ONSET ALZHEIMER'S DISEASE. AS HER ILLNESS PROGRESSED HER SONS MOVED HER TO A SECURE FACILITY IN PORTLAND, OREGON. SHE DIED SIX YEARS LATER.

RUTH'S ACCEPTING SPIRIT MADE THAT LAST TERRIBLE JOURNEY A BIT EASIER FOR ALL OF US. SHE CONTINUED AS ALWAYS TO LAUGH AT OUR SILLINESS AND MADE GESTURES THAT TOLD US SHE WAS STILL INSIDE THERE SOMEWHERE.
AT LEAST I LIKE TO THINK SO.

SPECIAL THANKS TO THOSE WHO WORKED WITH ME TO PRODUCE
THE ORIGINAL BOOK. THEY INCLUDE, MELISSA MARSLAND, HELEN BYERS,
RUTH WOLMAN, PETRA MATHERS, MICHAEL MATHERS,
TERRY MELTON, NANCY COMBS, RUTH MCKINNEY AND BILL HAUGSE.

THANKS ALSO TO ROBERTA MILLER AND ADELE MENICHELLA FOR THEIR
STEADFAST ENCOURAGEMENT AND HELP ON THIS EDITION.

AND MY TECHNICAL ADVISER, CHAD ESSLY.

JOHN HAUGSE BIO

John Haugse is an award winning professional animator and film maker. He received a BFA from the Art Institute of San Francisco and an MFA from the University of Oregon. He has taught at Harvard University and numerous Universities in the Northwest. His honors include the John Guggenheim Fellowship and several Grants from the National Endowment for the Arts. More notes on his work and this book at "http://www.theartofjohnhaugse.com" www.theartofjohnhaugse.com John lives and works in Santa Barbara, CA.

Printed in the United States
By Bookmasters